First published in 2002 by Brimax,
An imprint of Octopus Publishing Group Ltd
2-4 Heron Quays, London E14 4JP

© Octopus Publishing Group

Created by Nimbus Books
Written by Lynne Gibbs
Illustrated by John Eastwood

A CIP catalogue record for this book is available from the British Library.

ISBN 1 85854 484 X

Printed in China

Mind Your Manners!

Contents

Good manners

Why are good manners so important? Well, unless you live on the moon or in a deep, dark forest, you will see other people everyday. So it is important for us to get along with each other.

What are good manners?

Is it enough to know which cutlery to use, or how to set out a "thank you" letter? Not quite. You also need to show consideration for other people, and to think carefully about how your actions may affect them.

Thanks Mum!

The people who care for you spend a lot of time making sure you have all the love and attention you need. Why not show them how much you care, too, by giving them a big hug and saying "thank you"?

Being polite and thoughtful

If you behave badly towards someone, he or she will feel miserable. So the next time you are tempted to forget your manners, stop and think for a second. Always try to be polite, thoughtful, and caring. You will be a much happier person, and so will others!

The benefits of good manners

If you have good manners, people will like being around you. And let's face it, we all enjoy company. There's nothing better than feeling that our friends and family enjoy being around us.

Also, by showing you care about other people, they will behave the same way towards you. Soon, you will find you have more friends and lots more people offering to do nice things for you, too. Now that can't be bad, can it?

Lucy and her brother Tom are going to help us learn about good manners.

The magic words

Let's start with the basics. You know, saying "please", "thank you", and "you're welcome". You'll be surprised by how much these little words mean.

Please

"I want a vanilla ice cream cone!" Now what kind of way is that to ask for something, hmm? Let's start again.

"Please may I have a vanilla ice cream cone?" Perfect! Now you have what you wanted, and the shop assistant is happy. In fact, she even smiles as she hands you your goods!

Always ask with a "please"

So the rule is whenever you are asking for something, start your sentence with the word "please". You will be amazed at how many people are impressed by your good manners.

Thank you

But wait a minute! When the shop assistant gives you your ice cream, you take it and walk out of the store without another word! Come back inside and see what you have forgotten. When you took your ice cream from the shop assistant, you should have said "Thank you".

You're welcome

You said the word "please" before asking for something, and then you said "thank you" when taking it. But now it is the shop assistant's turn to say something. When a person says "thank you", it is polite for you to then add, "You're welcome."

So remember

- "Please" when you want something.

- "Thank you" when you get it.

- "You're welcome" when someone thanks you.

- Even if someone else forgets their manners, still respond politely to their request.

9

Table manners

Having good table manners is important. After all, there is nothing worse than listening to someone slurping, burping, and sucking their way through a meal. So here is what you should do.

Sticky fingers

We eat most food with cutlery, but there are some foods that even your Mum will let you eat with your fingers. These include sandwiches, crisps, corn on the cob, and fruit.

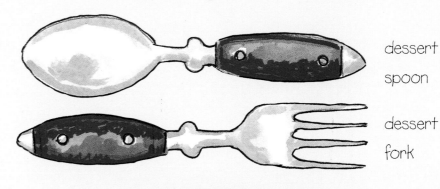

dessert spoon

dessert fork

bread knife

napkin

side plate

fork

plate

Cutlery chaos!

You've been invited out for a fancy meal, but when you see all the cutlery, you break into a sweat. Just which knife, fork, and spoon are you supposed to use first? Simple, start with the cutlery placed on the outside and, course by course, work inwards, then upwards.

Napkins

This may come as a surprise, but a napkin is not for blowing your nose, or hiding unwanted vegetables. It is for dabbing your lips! When you sit down, unfold your napkin and lay it across your lap.

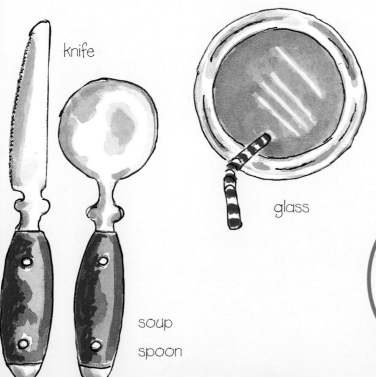

knife

soup
spoon

glass

Take a break!

You are not a hamster, so do not stuff food into your mouth until your cheeks are bulging. Take short pauses, placing your cutlery apart, at a slight angle on the plate. Once you have finished eating, lay the knife and fork (or fork and spoon) side by side, with the prongs of the fork pointing upwards. Did you know, it takes your brain 20 minutes to register that you're not hungry any more? So take your time!

Ultimate NO-NOs

Things you should NEVER, EVER do at the table:

- Take food from your neighbour's plate.

- Pick food out of your teeth with your fingernail.

Being respectful

If you treat other people the way you would like them to treat you, you will not go far wrong. Good manners are all about thinking about other people and being respectful.

Do not interrupt

It is rude to interrupt when someone is speaking, so wait until the person has finished before you butt in! If you need to speak to someone urgently (and "urgent" doesn't mean asking someone if they are leaving their fries!), gently put your hand on her arm and say, "I'm sorry to interrupt, but could I speak to you urgently, please?"

Sharing is caring

Don't be a greedy monkey! Just because Auntie Maud has given you a huge box of chocolates, it does not mean you have to scoff the lot! Offer them round! It would be a nice gesture if you offered them round BEFORE eating all your favourite ones! If you share your things with others, they will want to share their things with you, too!

Turn taking

No one likes a queue-jumper, so do not push in! It can be pretty scary, especially for elderly people, when kids push and shove each other to jump on the bus first. You may think you are only having fun, but other people may not see it like that.

Respect for others

If you push, shove, shout, interrupt, and refuse to share anything, why should others treat you with respect? So the next time you forget where you left your manners, apologise, and try to make up for your rudeness.

Ultimate NO-NOs

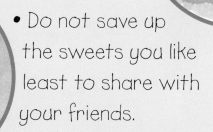

• Never shove someone out of the way to get the last seat on the bus.

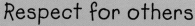

• Do not save up the sweets you like least to share with your friends.

• Never yawn or tap your feet impatiently, if you are bored by someone's conversation.

Everyday manners

Let's be honest, we all do it – burp, pass wind, and sneeze, that is. How many of us can say we have never, ever picked our noses? But there is a time and a place for everything.

Nose picking

If your nostrils need de-bugging, USE A HANDKERCHIEF! Do not wipe your nose on your sleeve, the tablecloth, or your best friend's coat!

Burping

You may feel better by burping loudly, especially after eating or drinking, but other people around you will not! If you cannot stop a burp from bursting out, then cover your mouth with your hand and say "excuse me" afterwards.

Passing wind

Now how can I put this politely? Let's say that you want to pass wind. What do you do? No. Letting it out and blaming the dog is NOT the answer! Go somewhere private, and then let it out. If you accidentally pass wind in company, do not blame the person standing next to you. Own up and say "pardon me".

Ultimate NO-NOs

Things you should NEVER, EVER do:

• Examine, or even eat, the contents of your nose.

• Sneeze, cough, or yawn without covering your mouth.

• Burp, even quietly, in someone's face.

Coughs and sneezes

Some people sneeze quietly, while others give great big, hurricane-style sneezes! But whichever way you sneeze, HOLD A HANDKERCHIEF OVER YOUR MOUTH. Other people do not want whatever is up your nose to be sprayed all over them! Sneezing and coughing are the fastest ways to spread germs.

Introductions

How do you introduce people? It is no use just saying, "Mum, this is Andy," because your mum will not know if Andy is a friend, neighbour, or someone you found in your wardrobe!

What's your name?

It can be difficult to know how to introduce family members, especially to a younger person. Do you say, "Mum, this is my friend, Andy. Andy, this is my Mum, Mrs. Sanders."? Or do you introduce your mum by her first name? To save embarrassment, ask your parents in advance how they prefer to be introduced.

Something in common

When you introduce people to each other, adding extra information such as where they are from, their job, or even their hobby can be helpful. This gives people something to talk to each other about.

Golden rules

If you remember two things, introductions will be simple:
• Always use both people's names twice. "Jenny, this is James. James, this is Jenny."
• Begin with the names of older people, women, high-ranking and important people such as teachers, politicians, clergymen, and even celebrities.

Proper forms of address

If you are introducing an older person or someone in authority, such as a teacher, you would say, "Mr. Mason, may I introduce my friend, Andy? Andy, this is my teacher, Mr. Mason." If someone has a title, always use it. For example, "Sir Elton, may I introduce Major Johnson? Major Johnson, this is Sir Elton."

Ultimate NO-NOs

Things you should NEVER do when introducing people.

• Get someone's name wrong.

• Only give one person's name.

Letter writing

There are many ways to get in touch with people, but receiving a letter is always exciting, isn't it? Different kinds of letters need to be written in different ways. Here are two examples.

The date goes here.

The greeting shows who is receiving the letter.

24 July 2002

Dear Mary,

It was really nice to see you last wee[k] had a great time at Susan's party and hope you did as well. I liked playing games and meeting Bonzo, the funn[y] clown best.

   I know your mum had a very long home after the party, so I hope you didn't get to bed too late!

   Don't forget that we have both been invited to Janet's party next Saturday. I can hardly wait!

Love,

Lucy

Set your letter in paragraphs.

A friendly letter

Your address goes here.

The recipient's address goes here.

Sender
Lucy Barker
35 Hewson Road
Bristol BS2 7HG

Mary Sullivan
30 Clarke Street
London E22 8PQ

Addressing an envelope

Write your address in the upper left-hand corner of the envelope. If the letter does not arrive at the address, then it will be returned to you. You can write the name of the city or use its abbreviation.

A formal letter

The address of the person receiving the letter goes below the date.

Tom Barker
35 Hewson Road
Bristol BS2 7HG

28 August 2002

Your address goes here, so the person receiving the letter knows where to send the reply.

Readers Book Shop
23 High Street
Bristol BS1 4DV

If you can find out the name of the person you are writing to, put his or her name in the greeting.

Dear Sir or Madam,

I am trying to purchase a book entitled "How to Eat Without Dribbling".

I wonder if you would be kind enough to let me know if you have a copy of this book for sale in your book shop?

I have enclosed a stamped addressed envelope for your rep...

Use a polite tone and plain facts in your letter.

Choose a formal closing.

Sincerely yours,

Tom Barker

Use your first and last names in your signature.

Don't forget the stamp!

Make sure you put enough stamps on your envelope. If you don't, the recipient (person you are sending the letter to) will have to pay the extra postage for you.

Phones and email

Thanks to the telephone and email, we can contact almost anyone in an instant! But remember, your voice and email may be the only impression a person gets of you, so telephone and email manners are very important.

Telephone tips

Before making a call, turn off background noises like the television or radio. When someone answers, give your name and the reason why you are telephoning. If the person you are calling sounds busy, ask if you can call back another time. Do not eat or drink while you are using the telephone.

Emails

Sending emails lets other people reply at a time that is convenient to them. Adding a smiley face is a sure way to cheer up friends! :) But remember, irony doesn't come across in emails, so avoid using it. Try not to use bold type or all capital letters – it comes across as if you are shouting . Also, don't send big files without permission – it can make some computers crash.

Mobile phones

Mobile phones are useful, but they can sometimes cause a nuisance to other people. Always switch off your mobile phone whenever you are:
• Inside a public building, such as a hospital, doctor's surgery, library, cinema, or at school!
• Speaking to other people.

Messages

Keep a notepad and pencil near your telephone so that you can take messages. If you leave a message, clearly give your name, telephone number, and a time when you can be reached.

Ultimate NO-NOs

Things you should NEVER do on the phone:

• Telephone early in the morning or late at night, unless you have been asked to or it is an emergency.

• Shout and laugh loudly into your mobile phone when you are in public places.

21

Party manners

All parties need some organizing. You need to make sure there is enough food and drink for everyone, the right kind of music to get people into a party mood, and plenty of games to play.

Sending invitations

A party needs people! There is no point giving a party if you do not tell anyone about it! Make a list of people you would like to invite. Then send out invitations. You can download some great invitations from the Internet!

What an invitation needs to say

An invitation needs to give the following information.

- Why you are having a party. Is it to celebrate your birthday, Christmas, passing an exam, or something else?
- Your name, contact address, and telephone number.
- Where your party is being held.
- The date and time of the party.

You are invited to a birthday party

by ...... Tom Barker ....

on ...... Saturday 20 June ....

at ...... 35 Hewson Road ....

...... Bristol ....

....
can/cannot come to your party
RSVP
Tom Barker, 35 Hewson Road,
Bristol BS2 7HG. Telephone 53607

Thank you notes

After a party, it is always polite to write a note to the host, thanking him or her for inviting you. (And that means even if it was the worst party you have EVER been to!) If you were the host and received presents, thank you notes are a definite must. Write down who each gift is from to include in your thank you note.

RSVP

To make sure people reply, telling you whether they can come to your party or not, write "RSVP". These letters stand for "Répondez, s'il vous plaît", the French words for "Reply, if you please".

Ultimate NO-NOs

Things you should NEVER, EVER do at a party:

• Forget to reply to your invitation and just turn up.

• Un-invite someone to your party.

• Discuss a party in front of children that have not been invited.

23

Good guests

Whether you are giving a party or just going to one, it is important to remember your manners. Even on relaxed occasions such as parties, people will still notice how you behave.

Being a good guest

The first sign of good manners is to arrive on time! A party is a time to have fun, but that does not mean at the expense of everyone else. So do not sing at the top of your voice to every record that is played.

Respect your host's home

Do not go into other rooms in the house unless you have been told it is okay to do so. Wait for the host to tell everyone when it's time to eat, rather than scoffing all the food on your own.

Being a good host

Make guests feel welcome by introducing them to each other. You will need to make sure they have enough food and drink throughout the party, too.

Any special requests?

If you have invited someone who has special needs, plan ahead and make sure you have catered for their needs. A vegetarian does not want to eat hamburgers, and someone who is in a wheelchair will not be able to walk up ten flights of stairs!

Party clothes

You should always state on invitations what kind of party you are giving. Is it a formal, informal, or even fancy-dress party? People will feel really stupid if they turn up in a smart outfit, when everyone else is wearing jeans!

Ultimate NO-NOs

Things you should NEVER do at a party:

• Have a food fight with the left-overs.

• Over-eat and make yourself ill.

• Leave without thanking the host.

• Say "Yuk" if you receive a gift you do not like.

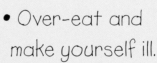

Good game!

After a game, how often have you heard someone say, "It's not the winning that counts, it's the taking part!"? You're right, the people who say that are usually the ones who have just lost! But if you take part in any game, you should always play fairly.

Being a good sport

Do not lose your temper or shout at the person or team you are playing against. Show you are prepared to lose as well as win a game, and with good humour. Never argue with a referee, they are only doing their job. At the end of the game, smile and shake hands with your opponent(s). (Okay, if you've lost, you can grit your teeth and mumble all the way home. After all, you're only human!)

Cheating

Even if you know that you are not as good as the other player, do not be tempted to cheat. Just do the best you can and remember that every time you play, you will gain more experience and become better at that game. Anyway, cheats are nearly always found out. Then you would be left feeling a real dummy, wouldn't you?

Team player

If you are playing in a team, do not try to take over the game! You may think you are the best player ever, but others will not see it that way. As part of a team, you all need to work together, each using your best skills.

Good spectators

Good sportsmanship should extend to the sidelines, too. If you're watching a game, don't be tempted to cheer when a contestant makes a mistake. And never shout out rude comments about your team's opponents.

Ultimate NO-NOs

Things you should NEVER do when playing sport:

• Trip someone up on purpose.

• Refuse to shake hands when you lose.

• Call your opponent names to demoralise or distract him.

27

Out and about

No matter how bright or funny you are, if you do not know how to behave properly, most people will only remember your bad manners! So it is no use giving your teacher an apple every day, if you then let a door swing back in his face!

After you

Holding a door open for someone else to go through first shows good manners. That does not mean you have to hold open a door until a long queue of shoppers has passed through! But if there are only a few people, hold open the door and politely say "After you".

What's the rush?

Running up or down stairs can be dangerous. You could trip and fall, or cause someone else to have an accident. Watch out for others and walk around people carrying lots of bags, or young children.

Being considerate

Good manners is all about thinking about other people and how your manners will affect them. For example, always walk, never run, through revolving doors. If a door is spinning around too fast, someone could trip and hurt themselves. And, if you see someone you know struggling with a heavy bag or case, it is only polite to offer to help.

Use the bin

How clean and tidy our streets would be if all the litter disappeared! So the next time you want to throw something away, look for a bin. That goes for your chewing gum, too. How would you feel if you sat on someone else's sticky, germ-covered gum!

So remember:

- Always offer your seat to the elderly, pregnant women, and people carrying lots of bags.

- Never swing your bag so it bangs into someone.

- Always use litter bins to throw away your rubbish and chewing gum.

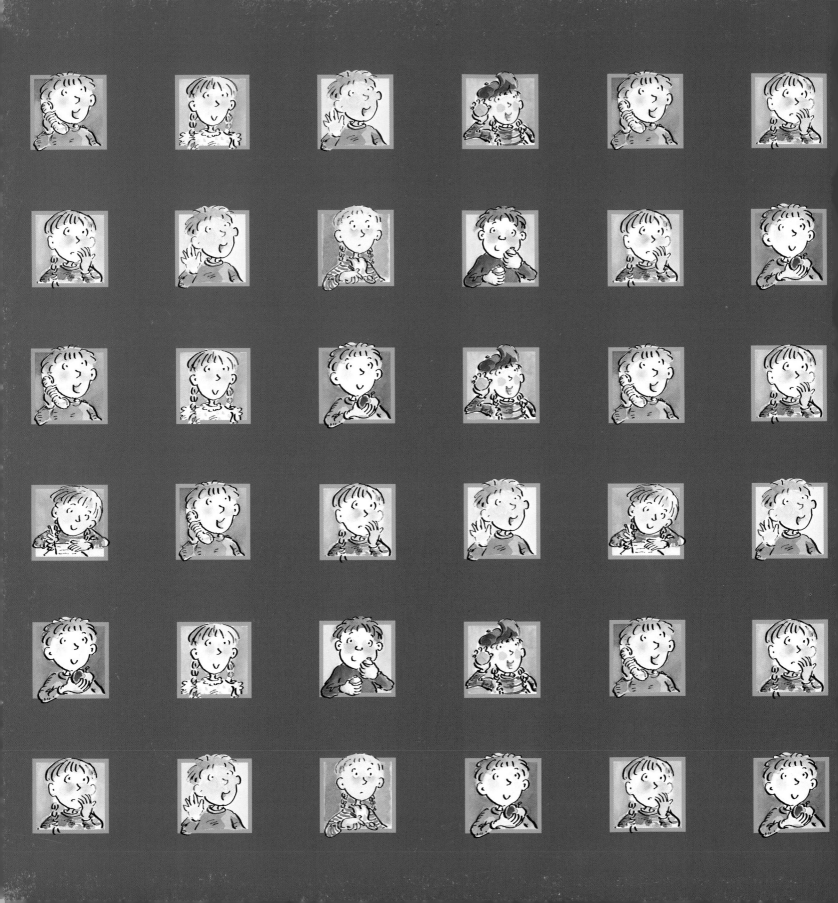